AT THE CORNER OF
FANTASY
AND MAIN

Disneyland, Midlife And Churros

Matt Mason

Cover and interior design by Nancy Levey-Bossert

Cover image: *Study of the Disneyland Castle* by George Scribner, 9"x 12" oil on Masonite, ©2022 George Scribner, used by permission.
Page 7, photo by Peggy Mason
Page 11 and 57, photo by Gordon Mason
Pages 35, 39, 45, 57, 65, 73, photos ©2022 Ted Kierscey
Page 77, photo courtesy the Wrather Family Archive
Page 78, Photo of Walt Disney courtesy of The Library of Congress

Set in Avenir Next, Ambroise Std Firmin and Coniferous used courtesy of Adobe Typekit. StarshineMF used courtesy of Richard William Mueller. New Press Eroded by Galdino Otten.

Printed in Korea
First Edition, April 2022

Hard Cover ISBN: 978-1-7357691-3-4
Library of Congress Control Number: 2021945414

Visit www.theoldmillpress.com

ACKNOWLEDGEMENTS

I owe thanks to the following periodicals and anthologies in whose pages these poems first appeared:

Briar Cliff Review: "What You Love"
The Carillon: "A Sort-Of Sonnet for Mid-Life"
Defenestration: "Karl Marx's Brain Explodes a Little by the Time He Hit the Churro Cart" and "Systematic Oppression and Goofy"
Green Mountains Review: "Disneyland, 2018" and "Space Mountain"
Lowestoft Chronicle: "You Turned Twenty-Five in EuroDisney"
Mousetalgia podcast: "The Dead Rewrite The Script," "Disneyland, 1979"
Plainsongs: "At the Corner of New Orleans and Frontier"
Small But Noteworthy: "When You Stayed"
Sugar House Review: "Certainty"
Thimble: "One of the First Places"

CONTENTS

FOREWORD

My greatest joy as an Imagineer was to visit the park and watch our guests interacting with the worlds we created, trying to imagine what they must be feeling. *At the Corner of Fantasy and Main* is a heartwarming and poignant exploration of those feelings – but not confined just to visits to the Happiest Place on Earth. Matt Mason is visiting our memories of the past as we search for reassurance in the present, all the while reminding us of our childhood dreams for the future. For those of us who have lived "a lovely life but have misplaced its key," Matt's poetry is a beacon of light in that search, beckoning to follow him around the corner and on till corndogs. I devoured the contents of this book like Matt devours his beloved churros.

-**Greg Combs,** *Imagineer 1990 - 2020*

DEDICATION

For **Mom and Dad**
And thank you **Sarah, Sophia,** and **Lucia**

Matt Mason- Disneyland 1979, Left.

FastPass to the Abyss

1.
This is a story
about midlife crisis,
this is a story without Ferraris
or affairs or movie clichés, this is a story

about Disneyland;
as, once upon a time,
a man turned forty-nine
and something changed.

2.
You slip
   out of bed,
   2am,
 to obsess over airfare for every hole in your calendar
these next eight months, you
did not
used to do this,
        your phone was not stuffed with podcasts
            named *Mousetalgia,*
            Connecting With Walt, Did You
            Know: Disney,

 and now, when
  your wife
    gets into the car with you,

     you change it to the radio quick,
       casual,
    Air Supply,
find yourself saying, *Ooh, yeah,*
 can't get enough
 I'm All Out of Love,
     can you?

Disneyland
is one thousand
five hundred
fifty-one miles away.
That's not so far, right?

You turn fifty next August.
Every thought
   did not used to be saturated with the Happiest Place On Earth,
   your head did not save so much space
   for Magic Kingdom trivia—you did not previously know
     that the park opened in nineteen fifty-five
     with a live broadcast's sugar smiles masking a meltdown
     of fake tickets doubling the number of feet sinking in soft asphalt,
did not know nothing
about Hatbox Ghost history
or that the Haunted Mansion was
modeled after the Shipley-Lydecker in Baltimore, Maryland
   or that there is a Disney park in Shanghai—what you feel
     is a tremor in your fault lines,
        this impending decline,
   the quickening slack
   of this mortal Slinky,

you did not expect
the form this Reaper takes:
FastPass for Space Mountain in one hand,
churro in the other,
mouse ears
set on his cowl,

he beckons
with so warm
a smile.

Disneyland, 1973

is so big, so much to see, so crowded so
you, so small, so four years-old, see mainly people's butts.
But so what, you
are wearing Mickey ears
with your name cursived on
by a sewing machine's golden thread, you

        are king
      of this castle
        poking in
    and out of view
  (between pants), you

rode a submarine, monorail, tea cup, elephant,
my God, cotton candy, Coca-Cola, popcorn,
your stomach feels full
of fireworks, please,

you can't leave,
  but, oh, man,
     just a minute,
        just a sec
            to lie down?

Matt Mason - age 4, Disneyland

The Web's Real Peril
—After William Carlos Williams

You have Google Flights updates, AirfareWatchDog, the
        Hopper app, you
have been going to Disneyland-
dot-Disney-dot-go-dot-com every day
to check for subtle differences in price, it
is more art
than science,
balancing the shades of airline miles, the mystery
        two-point-five-star hotel you can book for
        this low, low price.

This
whole thing
is not affordable.

You have kids
to take out of school
so you can take advantage of January
and its lower-crowd days,
you hide what you're working on
from your wife,
act busy, click
away from Mousesavers-dot-com
when you hear her approach, no,
hon, just immersed in this Buzzfeed article about
emojis, nothing to see here,
move along, please,
move
along

(because
you've booked
the flight home, but

not
the flight
there, so

much depends
upon

the web's
real peril,

crazed with shamed
shoppers,

behind the white
kingdom).

At The Corner of Fantasy and Main

You've got the castle's shadow,
not the castle, got mallards
looking for a moat, photographers
with poses to pick from
as horse-drawn streetcars clop by,
you've got donuts,
different every week,
sometimes a lemonade maple bar,
sometimes pineapple and pink
at the place where lands transition
from Photo Supply Co
to Bibbidi Bobbidi Boutique,
where you're never quite sure
the pinpoint, the border line
between where dust needs sweeping up
and where it makes you fly—
all you know
is that somewhere nearby
someone
always has the particular magic
that turns three bucks
into coffee
and a paper cup.

Flight

You
soar

with cartoon movie elephants whose ears
are wings, and

that's not so ridiculous,
you flew into LAX on a metal whale

way heavier
than any pachyderm

much less a baby one
with a small, pink circus hat;

you flew here
when you were a kid, too,

you remember this, now,
you fly with

your kids,
daughter

seated next to you,
recklessly steering you up

and down
as the world

keeps orbit
around

you.

Disneyland, 2015

It's significant,
the parent who returns with his mate and their children
like some nature documentary
calmly play-by-played in the narration:

> *And, as he came with his parents when he was small,*
> *he returns to this same spot with his young,*
> *teaches them how to hold a churro and*
> *not wipe grease on their pants, that, to survive,*
> *you need to get in line at the gate*
> *30 minutes before the park opens.*

> *The pack leader*
> *guides his family on an ancestral migration*
> *to navigate these lands of flying elephants*
> *and pirate caverns.*

Lucia
just wants the slide.
The one at the hotel pool.

I mean,
it's a good slide,

but
this is Disneyland
where there is a Destiny
of submarines, bobsleds, macaroons,
this

pool
is kind of similar
to the one at the Hilton
in Council Bluffs,
Iowa.

The narrator shrugs.
He starts making stuff up to keep the audience engaged.
Hopes
this all
works out.

A Sort-Of Sonnet for Mid-Life

It's not like you want or expect you'll live
    forever, it's just adjustment, to turn
the corner to a street that's elusive
    to describe—older? a little bit burnt?

There is brightness here, there's a majesty,
    oh, this age is just different, foreign,
though still home; stop seeing this as messy
    when it is much less mess than being born.

Still, forty-nine. You're overfilled with wants,
    a carry-on suitcase for a year's trek
    stuffed to the airline-limits of your head's
    capacity, wanting to bust free fast
    for any possibility, one hand
reaching, desperate, for the right doorknob.

Song of Your Churro

Life
would hold more joy
were a churro
in your hand—

no,

a churro
in your hand but
a bite
in your mouth, too;

a crunch, a star
on your tongue,
sugar,
cinnamon,

the rest, then,
in your hand
to punctuate:

exclamation mark
there to sing
its own
acclaim.

At Some Age

At some age
you wake up to discover
you are now an old orphan
with priorities unrecognizable
from the versions you imagined were
surely on their way;
you find yourself
chained to a small screen which won't stop ordering you around:
       go to this meeting
       and answer these emails
       and pick up kids
       and unload the dishwasher and
       load it all again and
       handle this calendar notification ordering you
          to roll a rock to the top of that hill;

wifi and electric dishwashers notwithstanding, this
is not culturally, societally new—
though
saying this
does
not
sooth.

You
have a lovely life

but have misplaced its key;

you retrace steps,
try to remember

where you last held it,
scratch at your pockets,

look
everywhere.

And this
can't be the end
of the poem;

this
is where there's supposed to be
some grace note of hope,

that closes the poem tight
with a soft bow
of rhyme.

Right?

Disneyland, 1992

You used maps, paper
maps to get here,
the kind you find
at interstate Rest Stops,
directions
laid out on sticky notes
pressed
onto colored roads and ranges,

and you were driving from one direction,
honeymooning friends from another,
you had uneven plans
made three states east
to meet
inside the entrance,
off to the left,
nine thirty a.m.
no cell phones,
no free-range internet,

but there's their faces,
they're still married, in this scene,
all the things to come
have not yet happened,
and Winnie the Pooh
bobs over to dance with all of you,
on this sun-hugged day
which has only just
said: ready,
set,

go

Tomorrowland, 1955

A vista into a world of wondrous ideas,
signifying man's achievements,
a step into the future, with predictions
of constructed things to come.
-from Walt Disney's dedication of Tomorrowland,
July 17, 1955

In its original design, Tomorrowland's setting was 1986,
chosen because it was the next return for Halley's comet.
-from *Walt's Utopia: Disneyland and American Mythmaking*
by Priscilla Hobbs

The world of 1986   as shown on black and white TVs
is all rocket ships   and small cars where Sammy Davis, Jr
can rear-end Sinatra, a place where atomic energy metaphor mouse traps
spray ping pong balls willy nilly;   Walt starts to talk,
then stops,   confused
as a voice in his ear tells him not yet   and Walt, broadcast live, waits.

Don't sweat it, boys,
take it from someone who graduated high school
in 1986,

you,
everything,
everything,
nailed it.

Space Mountain

gets tough
to get to
in the belly of the day,
but
when the Sun goes snuff
and the parade lights up,
you
sprint
the whole line, rockets
waiting for you like a valet roller coaster
again
and again,
scream
through the stars,
bolt out the exit,
shoot back through the queue,
arms
half-raised,
the galaxy's
ecstatic exhalation
against
your face.

Systematic Oppression and Goofy

What does Goofy think
when he sees Pluto
leashed
to that master?

Goofy
clomps in,
wearing pants,
car keys
chiming in a pocket.

Does he
look down
at the long tongue
of a cousin

and think
there
but for the grace of God,
hyuck?

Does he ever look at that giant
gloved hand, the fist
at the end of the leash,
and feel
his ears
pull back?

After Mom also dies, there are boxes of photos brought to your basement

When you look through, they're all over:
some in sleeves from different photo labs
and *Christmas 1974* penned
above a 30 Cents Off Developing coupon,
others unmarked,

stacks run loose in the box with birthdays
pressed against vacations pressed against Thanksgiving dinners,
color, black and white, some
with a border around the photo like they did in the 50s-into-70s,
an intimidating storm of the ages
of photo development;

and these,
marked *MAY 1973* along the white border,
you find three from Disneyland,
you are four,
you are wearing incredible yellow and navy plaid slacks,
Mom in a purple pantsuit, there
in front of Sleeping Beauty Castle, click,
King Arthur Carrousel, click, getting on the Santa Fe and
      Disneyland Railroad,
click, and you remember
none of it.

You wish you could see your dad.

He's the one
behind the Instamatic.
It's his eye
you look through
that keeps these scenes
alive.

Ode to Submarine Voyage (1959-1998)

This is the ride you remember vividly, though,
so many other parts of that trip faded since you were four,
but this ride still E-ticket in memory, asking Mom and Dad:
how did we end up so deep?

as if you had
all gone under the waves and down
to Atlantis' cracked pillars,
mermaids waving, undersea volcanoes,

the serpent's tail
that stretches and rolls on and on
to fill your imagination
with fierceness, with dragon fangs, but ends

on a gap-toothed conclusion, it
was the voyage for you,
the library book you loved to read
in bed, under covers, by flashlight,

wished you could fold yourself inside, so
your parents say
it was only illusion,
you didn't go far at all, but

you did,
you know
you went down under Tomorrowland's oceans and ice caps,
in with the squids,

down
to the dark
start
of worlds.

Memory

Memory is thing
is object is possession
is grey cell fed oxygen drop
is electric jolts passing notes down the line.

Memory is brain is relative
to the bomb pop, Monorail stop, the Huffy with banana seat,
Ho Hos in foil wrap,
not spirit, not quintessence, is particle
is zero is one is data logged in skull box,

so, afterlife you, what are we,
what afloat in what wafts past clouds,
what identity, what daughter's eyes wide open as you see her
born, what Mom's words when you both bump into
      John Lennon in an elevator, what sounds, what sparks,
what minutes drip back to dirt
as cell walls crumble to sluice,
as nucleoli spill

                  to szzzzzzzzzzzzzzzt;

memory is thing is drip, drip, drip
   is vocabulary on the shelf since sixth grade science class is what
isn't what we are is peanut shell is dust is VHS video tape of 1977
       Star Wars
 is Library of Alexandria
   is Codex of the Maya
is Dead Sea Scroll sieve
 is pulled out in our wallet is
matter, doesn't
       matter in the eternal
        in what comes
  after the flood,
  the fire,
 the ice,
the Ragnarok,
the Armageddon,

     these
     words
     we'll forget
     when stripped
        to
     stars.

One of the First Places

When both your parents were dead,
you took your wife and daughters to Disneyland.

There's a family trip
when you were four
that you remember—

not so well
with your head, it's
one of the things
inside you,
old sparks
still warm
in your wires.

You don't pretend to know what is
sensible under these circumstances, what is
reaction and what is
accident when such normal
but extraordinary things happen
and leave your life
as something you don't recognize.
You miss them.
You're looking for them.

This is one of the first places
you remember seeing them.
Maybe
something's still there.

At the Corner of Fantasy and Frontier

There are streets you never knew,
small door out the castle
which winds to a cobblestone village nook
on to tacos and rifle range and giddyup guitar.

Pathways pop into existence
that weren't here before,
they change the maps
as they go,

string connections between ideas
as sure as paved metaphors
for lands you know
must be connected but couldn't see how,

these rabbit holes, flying ships,
second star to the right
and on
till corndogs.

Karl Marx's Brain Explodes a Little
by the Time He Hits the Churro Cart

It's so America,
so nineteen fifties,
so Main Street nostalgic, so
Karl-Marx's-brain-would-explode-by-the-time-he-hit-the-churro-
      cart capitalistic.
You suspect he'd prefer the Mickey beignets.
You remember when Nemo was a Captain, not a fish.
You remember running into Winnie the Pooh
inside the turnstiles and to the left,
at the spot set to meet old friends.
It's a thrill to be back now, bring your nuclear American family:
your oldest wants the Matterhorn,
your youngest wants the Dumbo ride,
your wife wants Peter Pan's Flight, you
just want everything, sugar
sprinkled on top,
leaving more dollars
at every stop.

Were Karl here, you could map just where his brain
would pop
(mapping his path past the hat shop the coffee shop the bakery
      shop the coffee stand the balloon seller the turkey
      leg shop),
you could mentally set an X by the churro cart as the farthest
      he could possibly get.
He would point out every child
crying in the line whipped around the Matterhorn,
say only, *See?*
he wouldn't need to preach,
just point,
curl his lip a practiced touch.
He wouldn't ride anything,

just stop at every cast member
and interrogate them (If you were watching from a distance,
you'd just see a lot of facial hair and a dusty suit
flapping and staring into a seventeen year old's eyes,
who, all of them, smile, shrug, continue
sweeping cobblestones or making Dole Whips or asking if they
    can take your picture).
The guy in the Goofy costume would sit with him at a patio
    table outside Jolly Holiday,
gigantic head bounding up and down like a diving board
    wearing a tiny hat
before he stands up, shakes a floppy shoe
and hugs a little girl in Mickey ears.

You pass him
on your way
to Pirates.
He's holding a corn dog,
his head cartoonishly oversized,
a triumphant grin painted on his mouth.

Mr. Toad's

is a Hell
of a ride
which
is unexpected
at Disneyland,
you don't anticipate
damnation,
of all things,
coming, it's
an unusual
end
for a cartoon
ride (heat,
demons,
steam
hissing
through the air),
especially
when that's
the happy ending
or,
not so much, but,
still,
the end
before
your motorcar rolls
back
to sunlight,
cool air,
to your heart
fast
as you tumble
out
amongst all
the choices
you've made
so far.

It's Complicated, Getting From "it's a small world" to Splash Mountain at One in the Afternoon

Your feet already hurt
and the ducks are swarming
like vampire mallards,
it's early July,
a Tuesday,
but that doesn't make a difference
as you can't take three steps
without a stroller the size of the Mark Twain Riverboat
cutting you off;

in the narrowest channels,
a group like these six friends in matching blue t-shirts
must make a sudden stop and stare at their phones, when,
for gosh sake, there are foot traffic rules
but you're in Disneyland,
you just purse your lips
and wedge your way around
(without the Side-Eye-Of-Justice
you burn
to give),

you'll hit
an open spot or two
you can slide through,
these
are magical,
decorated
for effect
with the shine of bubbles
from a kid's Mickey bubble shooter

before it's back to the strollers, the ducks, the gathered
        hordes walking six abreast
like they're in a race against a hare and are, at this point
        of the story,
spelling out the moral to a T:
Slow and steady
wins the race.

You've got a FastPass for Splash Mountain
that expires in a couple minutes
and you don't know
if you're going to make it
and   that churro cart there
is   giving you a come-hither look
and   you find yourself standing
in   the narrows of a walkway,

not sure what to do
as grumbling crowds
rocket
around
you.

At the Corner of New Orleans and Frontier

Under Old West guitar and Jazz band trumpet,
where the riverboat steam horns blare,
you order a corn dog.

Beignets and étouffée
are down the way, cowboy,
you don't have to put up with that.

But the sun dips into everybody's eyes,
strollers full of screams rock by
and you

need to start searching, at the popcorn cart and in your life,
for something more
than everything

you've been settling
for.

Poem Review Composed on Disneyland's Pirates of the Caribbean

So
you ride a boat
through a New Orleans-themed restaurant,
nobody barely looks up
from their Monte Cristo sandwiches,
guy pulls at some banjo strings,
in sync with the crickets
as your boat rolls past;
around a bend, a skull wearing a hat
says something,
but before you can gather what he's trying to tell you,
the bottom drops
to waterfall splash, and
robot skeletons (or
are they droids? You forget the right name)
tell you all sorts of tales
while telling you
they don't tell tales
(but that's a storyteller, you suppose,
they tell you tales
about not telling tales in their tales);
skeletons situated
on Matterhorns of gold, relaxed in dusty beds, they
tell more tales, they
grow faces and shoot
at you, at each other, at everything
as cannons steam and things like "Davey Jones!" gets
            dropped in conversation, you
chug into a little town
overrun by droids and Johnny Depps,
but everyone seems to want the red-haired pirate woman
            more than Johnny Depp,
except for the pirate
who looks at his pig friends

the way we all wish Johnny Depp or a red-haired pirate woman
would look at us;
and there's up-tempo singing with a donkey and a dog
all while the town burns down
and there is shown an alarming lack of footwear;
here, the dog's the smart one,
he's the one outside the cage, he's got the keys, waits
for the best offer as the charred logs groan
and the audio-animatronic pi-robots (that's
what you'll call them!)
give a PSA on how too much rum has a real impact on your
        decision-making skills as
Johnny Depp sings
and you get whiplashed
by boat after boat rear-ending,
and a maritime escalator carries you back, yo ho yo ho,
to where it all starts
again and
again and
again.

The Dead Rewrite The Script

Now I will raise the safety bar
and a ghost will follow you home.
　　　　-from the end of the Ghost Host's
　　　　Haunted Mansion spiel

But you know the ghost won't.
And that's not science
where you can dismiss the paranormal
as a Pepper's ghost who pops
if the light bulb does,
electric spirits spun in the same story
every minute of the Park hour,

this is about grim grinning ghosts
come out to socialize,

and halfway on the walk to the Hyatt,
their eyes'll be rolling far enough back
to see out their top hats,

these creepy creeps dig
a swinging wake

and all you're up to
is staring into a little screen,
talking about some sports thing, or
writing a poem;

grim
grinning
ghosts
don't come out for this.

And
until further notice:

if you don't start behaving
with a little more liveliness,

they won't be caught dead
with the likes
of you.

The Lilly Belle

is a train car
people go ga ga over
because Walt
and Walt's wife Lilly
and you get the picture, right,

there are decades
of connections here
to trace and track and steam along,
from the original little engine he gave her
to this plush caboose you can ride
at very certain times
that you'll see hooked up some mornings
and gawk and pull your phone out
for a blurry photo from too far away

before she disappears
for the day, as
they say young Walt ran alongside the trains back in Missouri
like something out of a movie,
that Mickey was born on one,
that Walt set tracks around his Land
like a wedding ring, that

if he was to show his love, this
is the gift
he'd give.

The Story
-At the Walt Disney Hometown Museum,
Marceline, Missouri

The story is that it was an old cottonwood
finally knocked dead by a lightning bolt a few years ago, but

in whose shade Walt Disney bloomed
into an artist, his belly botany and storytelling,

his ideas scratched
with chalk

then brushed
to dust

to start again
and again

there in the unrushed peace
of a kid,

his back to the bark
as cardinals and crickets sang.

And at the gift shop, you bought a chip of its wood,
button-sized,

and it reminds you of the thorn
your mom held like treasure in a glass box on a tray,

she bought it on a street in Turkey before you were born;
the man told her it was a rarity,

a relic
from The Crown of Thorns.

We
buy thumbnails of miracle,

pay for more than fragments,
than diadems of atoms,

we pay
for the story

to watch over us,
to guide us

past cottonwood tops,
past lightning,

past gravity,
past skies.

The Birth of Mickey
-At the Walt Disney Family Museum,
San Francisco

When it starts,
a couple guys on a train
mess with a blank page,

draw what they call mice,
but
who's ever seen a mouse like that?

Those ears
are more
cymbals, satellite dishes, moons,

but
when the guys get home,
they keep going

with sketches
scratched, experiments, each one
a little different,

they're fun/funny, but
nothing you'd dream
will grow up to be

movies
and watches
and Disneylands.

It's just pencil marks,
a couple figures circled
as, hey,

that's an ok look,
run with that,
find him the right name,

what could it hurt?

At the Corner of Fantasy and Tomorrow

There are turkey legs for sale.
They're huge.
You think you're that hungry.
You're not, dude.

This is the sort of decision you carry
from Land to Land,
from popcorn cart
to churro stand.

There's a reason
the prince and princess
are never shown
grown fat:
someone types *Happily Ever After*
and just leaves it
at that.

Reflections of William Blake's Watercolor
The Expulsion From Eden

You visualize the red horses
whose riders are fire,
the pale angel
who grasps Adam and Eve's wrists
while they have their free hands up
as if about to slap at the angel's grip.
They stare down the serpent
under the angel's heel as they, barefoot,
step, for the first time, onto thorns.

It's similar to Michelangelo's *The Fall and the Expulsion*
where an angel presses his sword to Adam's skittish neck
while he and Eve turn to flee, less dramatic
than Benjamin West's, more like Doré's engraving, maybe,
and it reminds you, too, of Cibot's *Fallen Angels*,
the way two slouching former-heavenly beings look
like they're about to sneer themselves
into leather jackets and a pool hall,
light up, cause trouble.

For some reason
these cross your mind
as you sit down
with a box of fast food chicken
on layover
in the Las Vegas airport,
headed home
from Disneyland.

You turned Twenty-Five in EuroDisney

Like in a fairy tale, there was a magic gift
(a bank's random drawing) and there was love;

the memories, though, the details
are as gone now as the dress from a fairy godmother when
      11:59 ticks to 12

without clock chimes, just digital silence,
a few thousand midnights
each taking a thread
away.

At most, there's one glass slipper left
among mice and pumpkins and old torn things;

you mainly remember her,
a breakfast where Goofy toppled comically,
a cake of indeterminate flavor,
twenty-five candles in it.

What sticks
is how much is missing. Even
her
who you loved.

When there's not
enough magic,
you both know, to make what doesn't fit

fit,
you have to show patience, have to know
you don't break up in Disneyland
you wait, like a script,

for a dark hotel room out in Paris,
calm conversation,
then a flight alone,
airplane seat tray table

you will watch
like a TV screen gone static but you're too tired to change it
for hour
after hour

half
your life
ago.

If You Have Survived This Far

If you have survived this far,
gotten to the later chapters of the book,
you will have lost some things
along the journey.
Some hope,
here; some dreams, there; joy
has become an afterthought;
you've seen both parents go,
so many obituaries and suits that don't fit you with any comf●
father bird flying for your others.
   Build
a fire
in the living room—
keep water handy, a fire extinguisher,
rainfall and river—
let it burn green,
take it
in,
spoon
by spoon,
to the blue part,
past it,
burrow to the yellow, orange, red tongues,
take them in,
fill yourself, stir
the ash.

     Tell me
what you find there,
what is it
you need, what
will bring you
back;
it may not
take shape
in ways
you anticipate,

but,
who's to judge
the place
you find
to start?

What the Shadow Doesn't Say Back

Shadow like smoke but
moves water to the touch, never
says, ignores your
words, hopes you'll leave it.

You're at the table,
laptop, email, spreadsheets, shadow
bored,
can't stop sitting, wishing
you'd go,
do something
different,
smoke stare
around the room,
its head
sideways
on the table
like a kid
begging
for the
new,
waiting
for its Peter Pan chance
to run.

Keats Never Mentions Disneyland

-after *Endymion* by John Keats

He had other things on his mind.
Still,

he tried to fashion beauty

in the hope
that this would be enough

to move away that cloud
which darkens spirits.

He threw words

like a man who blows dandelion fluff at a dragon's snarl-
        sharpened maw
and stands, head high
with the certainty
that this
is enough.

Keats died with only twenty-five years in his pocket.

Now he's the one
painted on a vase, unable to age
another day as his bright shape intimates

that *a thing of beauty
is a joy forever*.

You feel fairly certain
that he was not referring
to a churro with those lines.
At least not specifically.

Still, there's a sign
as you enter Disneyland: *Here*

you leave Today

and enter the world of Yesterday,
Tomorrow and Fantasy. Keats

lives in all of these

and, you think,
he might call it beautiful

if he could come out
from behind that biography you had to memorize

for tests in high school, take your hand so you could pull him forth
and show him this carousel,
steamboat, Paris daisy,
jacaranda, submarine,
pink trumpet tree, space rocket,

as your life hits its stride,
you blessed child, young man, father of almost twice Keats' years,

what dreams do you still carry with you,
what dreams do you dream next,
what dreams do you hold before you
to dispel this immortal despondence?

At the Corner of Adventure and Frontier

At the corner
of Adventure
and Frontier,

where wisps
of pineapple frost
rise in crests,

where there are lines of people
on either side of a tiki counter,
sits your dad's ghost,

blue and white flowers
in full bloom
on his shirt from the island where he was born.

He is a spirit
on a bench
next to a giant bird of paradise tree.

Your oldest daughter sits down with him, her hands around
          a Dole Whip cup,
though you don't think she sees him:
she is in stillness,

eyes closed,
approaching this universe
like a hibiscus

in
full
bliss.

Disneyland, 1979

You find a photograph
            in the box,

you don't

            recall
                any,

your dad leans against a white rail,
he smiles
                    with you,

        Monorail track
                    in the background, and

            you don't
                remember;

how
        does this
        exist only

  on this
        paper square
        in a yellowing envelope
        marked with a year which
        if you lost this chip of it
        would wholly
        disappear?

Certainty

You were in Disneyland
months ago, haven't
deleted the app yet,

check, now and then,
for the wait time
on Big Thunder Mountain Railroad,

even though
you're in line at McDonald's
in Omaha.

You could be in the Haunted Mansion
in thirteen minutes
if you weren't.

You
wonder
about your arteries.

You pay for a Quarter Pounder,
ponder the inevitables
of Death

and Taxes and
the line for Peter Pan's Flight
is forty minutes long.

When You Stayed

When you stayed
at one
of the Disneyland Resort hotels,
you left with
twelve small soaps.

Ah, small crime,
for months
you'll leave behind
hints
of mint and rose.

Mr. Toad's Wild Rhyme

You're just another aging man
growing brittle, out of shape,
preoccupied with Disneyland.

Another day without a plan,
another stumble, misstep, mistake
for just another aging man

looking for something more grand
than emails and meetings and frustration,
so you're preoccupied with Disneyland

where Yesterday, Tomorrow, and Fantasy
are supposed to replace Today
for just another aging man;

and maybe that's survival, necessary sleight-of-hand,
salvation in escape
in preoccupation with Disneyland

on a wild ride that maybe will only complicate
your comprehension of obsession's weight
when you're just another aging man
preoccupied with Disneyland.

Disneyland, 2018

Your youngest,
throat went wrong days before you left, wobbled off balance,
      recovered

just in time
to be the only functional one of you,
your wife staring through you all as if you are ghosts,
you hoping that these feelings
are not about vomit

(It is sadness
to acknowledge
that if one eats anything
shaped like Mickey's head,
there will be
repercussions).

Your oldest hasn't left the hotel room,
she groans in the day bed,
does homework
from the classes she's missing.

You,
in slow motion, day
by day have
blossomed into cough, sniffle, groan,

your youngest dances,
she is the generator
who could juice all of Space Mountain
and more,
she asks questions, bounces bed to floor to bed to floor,
the sinus
behind your right eye
slowly cracking the walnut shell of your skull;

your wife stares,
small twitch
and sigh,

you
feel like the poison apples
in the Happiest Place on Earth,
the ones
who bring this all
down.

At Disneyland, She's Excited

the hotel swimming pool has a slide.
This thrills her
more than anything with a line to get into.
She loves her new swimsuit,
palm trees, she's seven,
she is unfamiliar with budgets,
with working extra jobs for airfare, park tickets, room
        reservations, food.
She knows
the poolside bar serves lemonade and pretzels;
she knows
how to lay back on the yellow curve
and speed down a ride punctuated with a
splash!

But does anyone need
to apologize
for knowing
everything
they want
from this bright,
sun-soaked
now?

What You Love

You won't feel alone,
though you meander
by yourself this trip,
these Lands set
like dioramas of your past:

Mom and Dad as they take you
on that submarine back when it was gray instead of yellow,
brother still in a room at the Disneyland Hotel because of
        chicken pox spots popping,

late night Space Mountain runs with newlywed best friends
back inside fairy tale days,

your oldest's first ride on the Matterhorn,
your youngest's first ride on Space Mountain,
your wife, face splashed with fireworks;

you walk through this park slow, move
like a leaf on a stream;

there are no work reports due today,
no updates or phone calls, just
joy

filling you like a gas tank,
like a reservoir,

something you didn't realize
you'd let go
so dry.

At The Corner of Frontier and Critter

Tom Sawyer Island's nature trail,
is fence lizards and orb spiders and butterflies,
cedar, sweetgum and acacia
watered with the screams
of Splash Mountain's last roar
across the rivers.

This calm
pirate's lair,
this dirt path
through the wild
both real
and engineered
so well you don't care
to know
which
is what
is which

out
where there are no waits,
no rush,
just paths
and caverns
and shipwrecks to explore.

Every Parade

no matter how firework
how tuba
how lit up digital slideshow
how churro and balloon
no matter how loud

it ends
with boom
with gasp
with hands
with claps
it ends

then brooms
say sweep
say sweep
say sweep

What You Find At Disneyland Is

that when you come here on a trip by yourself and investigate why you can't stop thinking about the place and had thought maybe it was the park itself and Walt and all his stories is that you were wrong and you're here because of you and all the stories you've been part of on trips made here in past years to this cheerful once upon an orange grove, and it's like pulling out boxes from the basement and trying to fit into clothes from different ages of your life and you can't with them small or faded or so brittle they splinter apart like straw or just out of fashion because you can't be four or twenty-five or forty-six ever again, you have to walk with one stiff elbow, the toe and heels that hurt, all these small pains that now take ages to soothe, you can't change any of this except maybe that gut but, man, you've come to exactly the wrong place for that when there are churro carts, peanut butter dipped in chocolate, a thousand sweet things shaped like Mickey Mouse's head, there is a legendary sandwich you find to be ham and cheese wedged inside of something more funnel cake than bread, you came here to ride Space Mountain and find answers but the answers aren't on roller coasters, they're in the rhythm of your body's aches as you hike up Disneyland Drive thinking about trips with your daughters, wife, parents, friends you find yourself walking without, here in the middle of your life, halfway to the next: Don't you dare waste a breath.

At The Corner of Adventure and Main

The park has been open fifteen minutes
and you're writing a poem
at a table at Jolly Holiday
while bright crowds flow
to the far-flung lands off the hub

and you're writing a poem
at the precise time
where you're not supposed to sit at a table, you
are supposed to get your ears on
and fly through the shortest lines of the day,
enjoying things before
more people squeeze in
and Indiana Jones takes 75 minutes to get to
and parents pushing strollers start to simmer.

It takes effort.
Writing a poem. See,
it builds muscle.
Metaphorically.

The horse-drawn trolley clangs,
the deep bass of one of the Tiki Room's pre-show rundown
        voices rumbles
and Main Street's speakers play brass band pep of
        "In The Good Old Summertime"

as bright crowds flow
and house sparrows chirp
and nobody's kids have been scolded yet.

All around you,
the day starts up
like a hand-crank music box
with those first
slow,
sweet
clanks
of song.

Yesterday's Heat

Your daughter's asleep in the room
and you're out at the poolside breakfast buffet
and that sounds more elegant than it is,
"Poolside breakfast buffet," as it's three kinds of bread,
a bowl of hard boiled eggs, an artful stack of bananas,
and family-friendly nineties pop.
The place is packed.
They're all here
to get fueled for a day at the park.
Your daughter and you will fly home today,
you're in no hurry, appreciating
the granddad with a hat like Goofy's face hanging over his own,
the sparrows who sing and dive for crumbs, kids
with mouse ear hats and princess dresses ready, yesterday's heat
washed back into the night
as today
gets ready
to show us all
something new.

Walt Disney relaxing in his office on May 23, 1955, several months before the opening of Disneyland.

BIOGRAPHY

Matt Mason is the Nebraska State Poet and is the recipient of a Pushcart Prize and several book awards. Through the US State Department, he has run workshops in Botswana, Romania, Nepal, and Belarus. Mason's work can be found in The New York Times, on NPR's Morning Edition, in American Life in Poetry, and a few hundred other journals and anthologies. Matt is based out of Omaha with his wife, the poet Sarah McKinstry-Brown, and daughters Sophia and Lucia.